SONGS FROM TWO CONTINENTS

Moris Farhi

Songs from Two Continents

Poems

SAQI

ISBN: 978-0-86356-408-6

This first edition published in 2011 by Saqi Books

A full CIP record for this book is available from the British Library.
A full CIP record for this book is available from the Library of Congress.

Printed and bound by CPI Mackays, Chatham, ME5 8TD

SAQI
26 Westbourne Grove, London W2 5RH

www.saqibooks.com

TO NINA

You are at my side
wherever you are!

Contents

Foreword

by Talât Sait Halman

Moris Farhi is a master-poet of sublime love and its erotic eruptions. He revels in the excitements offered by a compelling woman – or womanhood – but is so enamoured by the seductiveness of lyrical language that balladry could be taken as his first love. Farhi is "the Henry Miller of poetry". His is the wisdom of sensuality.

As a virtuoso of the English language, Farhi is a marvel. Like Vladimir Nabokov, he excels in the fourth language he has mastered. He was born into a Jewish family in Ankara, Turkey, where he was initially exposed to Ladino (Judeo-Spanish), Turkish and French. He began to learn English as a teenager at Istanbul's Robert College, the oldest American educational institution outside the USA. His training at London's Royal Academy of Dramatic Art from 1954 to 1956 helped him to adopt English as his literary vehicle. Today, one wonders how a latecomer can achieve such an impeccable style in his fourth language.

After a brief stint as an actor and a successful career writing for television, he embraced fiction, a dedication that earned him acclaim in the UK and many other countries. His six impressive novels – *The Pleasure of Your Death* (1972), *The Last of Days* (1983), *Journey through the Wilderness* (1989), *Children of the Rainbow* (1999), *Young Turk* (2004), and *A Designated Man*

(2009) – along with international awards, fortified his literary reputation.

Farhi's fiction, which spans diverse cultures and countries in Europe, Latin America and the Middle East, depicts the trials and tribulations of individuals beset by hostile forces, yet brave enough to withstand and prevail. *Young Turk*, consisting of thirteen tales that evoke his native Turkey, unfurls dramatic events and touching human episodes at a time when the Turks were providing a haven for European Jews whose lives had been jeopardized by the Nazis. In *Children of the Rainbow*, Farhi deals both with the Nazi policy of extermination of the Roma and the prevailing demonization and persecution directed at them today. *Journey through the Wilderness* is a masterfully blended account of the South America's realities and mythology. *A Designated Man*, his latest novel, is a gripping story of blood-feud and its impact on the future of a quasi-utopian island. It stands as a parable for the endless conflicts of our times and advocates reconciliation through tolerance and love of the "other".

In all his novels, Farhi places innocent individuals in an inimical society and forces them to struggle against injustice and brutality. The dominant mood is revulsion that evolves into sorrow or spleen. Yet, no Farhi novel ends in despair or darkest pessimism.

Now, after nearly four decades of fiction, Moris Farhi returns with the present book to his first love. Not that he had ever abandoned writing poems. In fact, most of the poems that appear here were published in a variety of literary magazines and journals.

Significantly, this first collection of poems is entitled *Songs from Two Continents*. The title strikes me as making a reference less to two geographic regions and more to sets of binary opposites expressed metaphorically, e.g. body and soul, life or death, reality and imagination, evil versus goodness, hatred versus love ... Farhi's "continents", in the abstract, are two poles apart. But, my feeling is that he proclaims in his poetry the victory of the good continent over the evil one. The convergence of two opposites, especially when the body and the soul merge to create paradise on earth, thus allowing sensual life to challenge death, creates an ultimate triumph and engenders powerful optimism.

Farhi has faith in "passion redeeming the loss of innocence" and sexual prowess not only for taking revenge against death but also for enabling humankind to attain scales of sanctity. Many of his poems, notable for their honest explicitness, sing paeans to the triumph of Eros over Thanatos. For him, *l'homme moyen sensuel* has hope for salvation only through love – neither spiritual nor mystical, but physical. *Simplismus* is the quintessence of the panacea he offers:

> "the deathless world he would create
> simply
> by making love"

Farhi's poems are alluring also for their *claritas* and *lux*. Not only in his erotic verse but in his entire poetic output, Farhi's aesthetic preference is for clarity and light. They have primacy in his strategy of apotheosizing womanhood as well as his beloved woman.

Brevity is essential for Farhi. Few poets are as succinct as he is. His poems seem seductively naked as are his heroes and heroines in bed. No loquaciousness, no artifices, no embellishments. Everything Farhi describes, be it *deliciae generis humani* or his delight in the explorations of carnal love, has stark immediacy. The power of his sensuality shuns – even dispenses with – the seduction of death. This is evident in his charming satire entitled 'Claridges, London', as well as when he elevates physical love to metaphysical sublimity.

Farhi's narrative probity and occasional epigrammatic flair make one wonder if he has acquired – and maintained for good – a taste for Anglo-American Imagist poetry, without ever neglecting an affinity with the luminescence of the Turkish "social realists", who were immensely popular in Turkey during Farhi's childhood and adolescence.

Pervaded by striking love poems, *Songs from Two Continents* must also be extolled for a few elegiac verses written for Farhi's wife Nina, who passed away in 2009. His 'Farewell gift (On the death of my wife and soul, Nina)' is a devastatingly poignant and dignified elegy that is bound to endure as one of the best of the genre.

Farhi's 'Linguacide' (presumably his coinage for killing the language or language genocide) is a powerful indictment of the killing of writers by authoritarian regimes, a policy which seeks to consolidate the absolute rule of "dictators, racists, nationalists, zealots of war, false prophets". It stands as a testament to the humanitarian spirit and the love of freedom of expression that have moved Farhi to serve the literary world with remarkable idealism and unfailing energy as Chair of English PEN's Writers in

Prison Committee and later as Chair of International PEN's Writers in Prison Committee. Such successful services earned him an MBE (Member of the Order of the British Empire) and a Vice-Presidency of International PEN.

Songs from Two Continents includes numerous effective poems that enshrine Farhi's compassionate concern for justice, peace and international harmony on earth. His 'After Auschwitz' is a chilling evocation, 'Mother' a condemnation of concentration camps and crematoria, 'Time of the rodents' a phantasmagoria of brutality and massacre, and 'Ties of blood' a dirge for Middle Eastern tragedies. 'Tomorrow', the briefest of epics, reviews existence as civilization, religion, politics and armed conflicts propel humankind to a future that may never dawn. Lamenting the Holocaust suffered by the European Jews and comparing them to the atrocities of Bosnia, Rwanda, Kosovo, Chechnya and Darfur, he mourns the plight of all persecuted peoples.

Songs from Two Continents will probably bring new recognition to Moris Farhi as an exuberant poet of love and as an eloquent exponent, like Nâzım Hikmet and Pablo Neruda, dedicated to the cause of peace and justice in the world.

Paths to God

many paths lead
to God

mine is through
the flesh

On strawberry beds

you can laugh
in a million ways
I know

but I prefer the ring
when it is
anarchic

when you and I
pant
snarl
howl
on strawberry beds

and
your name
your earthy bouquet
your sexual sophistication
bestow upon the Bosporus its empyreal aura

Claridges, London

she was crying in my bed

she had
a home
a husband
children
security
insurance
money in the bank
food
clothes
car
cosmetics
clean sheets

and
status

all the items of love
she kept saying

but sex
once a month only
if she's lucky

Luck

Luck is not smiling upon us
they say
Fortune has gone to visit Mehmet
in the next village
and Reason's on a pilgrimage
they say

who cares

come
smile at me
with your breasts

Rebel

stop conforming
undress
lie down
with me
and rebel

A hungry queue

the blind man of the neighbourhood
the deaf man from the ferry
the hunchback on the 6.25
and my father's bank manager
the fat, the thin, the bald, the hairy,
the student, the baker, the coppersmith, the sailor
and the useless like me

queue
at the wrought-iron doors of a brothel
in the slums of Istanbul

Auld lang syne

the fish cemetery
the sea-burnt horizon
the sponge
the crab
and the slippery eel
recalled a miraculous time
as the wave broke on my head

as the wave broke on my head
I inhaled the stench of dead scales
and felt the pain of lost youth

I remembered the beach
and you and me
naked
as the wave broke on my head

Profanity

God and Nature
are married
they say

will He ever forgive
me
when I lie with Her
on the tideless Aegean
and drink from Her fount

The libertine's song

Come onto the beach
velvet skin
and I'll take you through time

I'll show you the reign
of the rose and the nightingale
limbs of lovers that rhyme

come on to the beach
velvet skin
come and lie on my purple and fine linen
I know so many love games
we won't know where to begin

Istanbul under the rain

dirty beautiful Istanbul under the rain
keeps me company
every night
on my way back
from
work
the tavern
or the brothel

there is an old secret
this magical city
keeps locked in her heart

the poor sucklings
of dear dripping Istanbul
are
ecstatically
unhappy

Tiredness

he got up
he washed
then he went back to bed

he thought:
it can only be love
that makes me tired
like that

Victual

mother and child
eat
the stench of rotting fish and onion peel
as they trudge
Istanbul's waterfront

Renunciation

woman
sweep me with
your whirling breasts
your liquid lips of desire
your wise eyes of abandon

carry me
to the perfumed dale between your legs

bury me
in your soil
woman

let me
at last
renounce the world
from within your earth

About death – I

he used to sit there
in the Bosporus café

it became a ritual with us
to smile, shake hands, exchange greetings
every morning before I boarded the ferry

Thursday he was not there anymore
he had seduced death the night before
as he had sworn he would

Revenge

he walked
dragging rusting iron feet
stopped
turned round to see where his legs had taken him
his eyes saw everything and nothing
he walked again
wondering where tomorrow might be
walked again

he murmured revenge

sulking clouds touched his hair
snow settled on his coat like dandruff
he was perspiring
the rancid sweat of the celibate

he muttered fiery words of revenge
he felt chained to a rock
the way they chain gods

he waited for his heart
to refuse
for once
for a minute

to refuse
to beat

he yearned for hot Mediterranean nights
blistering aquatic days
naked women
wanting him
him

wanting
his flesh
his cock
his semen
the deathless world he could create
simply
by making love

his leaden feet sank into the slippery asphalt
he groaned
and swore revenge

uprooted
all his life
uprooted
from
the past
the present
the future

uprooted
for
good reasons
bad reasons
no reason

he tried to understand
instead
he vowed revenge
revenge
for having had roots
for needing roots

he shouted revenge
for someone to hear
preferably a woman

man is what he makes of himself
I shall make myself ...

who was listening
who would listen
who could listen
who cared

women
all those women
he wanted

needed
who wanted him
needed him
whom he could love
who could love him

I shall make myself ...

he turned round again
the void nothing but the void
there are no tomorrows here
and no yesterdays
he walked again
dragging rusty iron feet

I shall make myself ...

don't say it, he hissed
don't tell anybody anything

let them try and guess

Ultimatum

don't give me
a handkerchief
a faded summer leaf
a photograph

to hell with symbolic love

give me
lips
neck
aureoles
arms
thighs
buttocks

order me
to expire
on your
Mount

Redemption

I can remember
the adult taste
of the quince
I shared with you
that conspiratorial day
when we followed the river
to the sea

I can remember
the confessional commitment
of our hands
as we kissed cheeks
innocently
beneath the silver olive tree

I can remember
being seven
wise as old wrestlers
and even wiser
about constant hearts

I can remember all that
today
as I lie in bed
a new woman tightly cradled on my chest
our juices the pool of a waterfall

I can remember all that
today
but I can't remember
your face
my first, my very first love

have you been loved
as I have been loved?
have you felt grace
when you blessed
your flesh
and not your mind?

does not passion
redeem
the loss of innocence?

Forget traditions

forget
romantic love
forget
traditions
principles
friends
family
beau monde

the sea is libidinous
there is madness in our blood

so come
on this carnal night
let us
lose ourselves
in
each other's
light

Thirst

drink me
you said
offering me your lower lips
soft
creamy
perfectly shaven

drink me
you said
where I am really a woman
and you will be a man

drink me
you said
where I cascade in waterfalls
and you will find God

drink me
you said
right there between my legs
drink me
my love
my love
drink me

where I am a fountainhead
and you will be redeemed

and I drank
and I am young
and I am a man
and I found God
and I am redeemed

but the thirst
dear love
the thirst

you did not tell me about the thirst
that is never quenched
that possesses one

you did not tell me
that I can never drink enough

The dowser

in Rumeli's shadow
death
voluptuous
waylaid me

she held me by the hand
my eyes scared lambkins
I pleaded

she whispered in my ear
my heart a hummingbird

I consented
she rubbed her breasts on my face
my mouth insatiable
I suckled

she opened her legs
my manhood a dolphin
I plunged

there in her well
I found
the only true water

Saturnalia

my protean island in the sun
sparkling like false teeth

my eternal virgin
curving your curves

we cavorted with bowlegged Mephistopheles
we ignored his sayings
and left a heritage
in blue Istanbul
that is waste
and triple waste

Leaving Istanbul

17:20
a pier
on the Bosporus

the sabre wind
the hidden sun
and me
alone

you
within a sigh's distance
already chained to
chaste thoughts

17:50
the ferry

jellyfish
waters where summer lies buried

you
at a window on the hill
teaching your lips
how not to kiss

and me
alone
womanless
death in my mind

18:20
Haydarpaşa
the train station
the steam
the tears
the bedlam of farewells

you
on crumpled sheets still fragrant with our sexuality
castrating desire
from your lusty limbs

and me
on the steps of the train
shadowing
the leopard-coat
the blond hair
the strong amorous legs

if I can sit next to her
the golden hair
the dolorous lips
the yielding eyes

the eager legs
might clasp me

between Istanbul–Sofia–Belgrade–Vienna–
            Paris–London
as you turn rusty and asexual
I might be redeemed
sucking lotus-growing breasts

Mother

graze the earth
fill your breasts
I need milk

Mother
bathe me in the light of the Moon
clothe me with the Sun
anoint me with life

Mother
stand in front of me
hide me between your legs
protect me from the oldest darkness

Mother
winnow the maize planters and the potato pickers
sift the weavers and the artisans
find me a sturdy spouse

Mother
raise the sap in the male
put growing greenness in the female
give me children

Mother
straighten my back
replenish my strength
your child is your child forever

Mother
close my eyes
open your flesh
take me in

Chinese whispers

Who says
death is better than sex

the dead
but who hears them

Royal guest

We are left with
hope
now
perhaps ...
someday ...
if ...
but
hope
is not
a stranger
in our house
we entertain him
royally

About death – II

why does a man have to die
leaving remains

if die he must
why not
incorporeal
like memory

About death – III

I'm wrestling
with death
but he's got
too many arms
why can't you help me
brother

About death – IV

is dust kind to man
are angels sensual odalisques
devils drinking companions

can death really be discreet
like unknown seas

Partings

there comes a time
when
I love
in fear

how many partings
can a man survive

There were days

Believe me
there were
days
when
the grass smelled like sea-sand
and the earth shuffled
softly, sweetly

there were
days
months
maybe years
when
people hummed
laughed
made love

believe me
there were such days
I almost saw them

Seed

children

I look into your eyes
and see
mother father brother sister wife
even myself

I look into your eyes
and see
my sons my daughters

can you
in my eyes
see
a father

can you
in my eyes
see
the love

it is not always seed that makes a patriarch

Journey's start

This is where we start
at the bottom of the abyss

we will journey
alone
until
you and they
join us

we will climb
the fires of the sky
we will scale
the darkness of the underworld

we shall not possess
earth to sit on
sea to wade in
there will be
only
the agony of kissing tears
the burnt boats
the beds of stone where we cannot love languidly

we will not stop
until
words can be spoken again
songs find the faith to be born
freedom is raised from its pit of cadavers

we will not stop
until
we reach
the rainbowland we promised our children

Armoured men

born
unborn
stillborn
children

are tossed this way and that

in this dungeon
where
armoured men
defend
country
faith
civilization

Letters to Asher

Dear Asher
my letters to you
for the week

Monday
I woke up
unemployment
still in my bed

Tuesday
I didn't wake up
I made love
all night

Wednesday
I wanted
endless cups of coffee
I had to have tea
I hate tea

Thursday
I tried to kill
time
but

time
runs faster
than I can

Friday
came too early
I wasn't ready

Saturday
Despair
sits
across the river
voluptuous
bare-breasted

Sunday
I rest
like the rest

First Commandment

and let us love
in abandon
not
as if our flesh
were broken pottery
and our juices
ash
it is not
in worshipping death
that we will forget
the many ways they have killed us
but
in embracing life

After Auschwitz

I have tried
like all fools try

I have tried
as best I could
to understand

surrendering
the courage to forget
to
memory's fury
I have tried very hard

here I try again

pen
paper
pencil
typewriter
words
alphabet
language
wisdom

their common link?
Communication

I know a secretary
who bites her pen

Another
who masturbates with a pencil

I know a journalist
who delights in raping virgin paper

Another
who charades crucifixion
and believes he is a saint

I know a scholar
who spits words
other people's

and a child
who hurls the alphabet
afraid
in revelation

I know
Hitler had a language
and it is claimed

he could ejaculate
I cannot
believe that

I know
each century
one man has wisdom

each century
only one man has wisdom

that man they say died in Auschwitz
but I refuse
to believe it

for I try to be that man

I have the answer
like every fool
I have the answer

love is wisdom
wisdom is love

who in Auschwitz
except the exterminated
could have known about love?

But who
on earth
could not have known about Auschwitz?

Time of the rodents

the army
with
a gargantuan appetite for souls
stops at a city
for rations

the inhabitants
are
herded
onto the fields

the men
are chopped
into ten pieces
(the general can only count
on his fingers)

the women
are left lying
legs still open
dead hands lovingly
clutching bayonets
the only pricks
that desired them

the children
are skewered
ten to a pole
(same general
with abacus fingers)

the army
runs out of
cities
and devours
its own souls

now
the rodents
surface

yesterday
they ate
onion peel
chicken bones
fish heads

today
the fare
is
multitudinous
endless piles
of

mutilated limbs
gouged eyes
torn tongues
rolled breasts
disembowelled trunks
severed genitals
pools
of
sweet
human blood

the rodents
revel
they are
the new masters
they have
conquered the earth
without lifting a finger

they knew man
better than
man knew himself

Ties of blood

FATHER
sprouted
from that shoot
of David
   which circumambulated Jerusalem's stones
   after the Dispersion
      which recognized Yahweh in all His other
      names
         which decked in Ottoman turbans helped
         raise the Levant as an ark for all races all
         cultures
            which shook hands with shepherds and
            artisans sipped tea with poets musicians
            and courtesans dressed janissaries and
            equerries waged war and peace on
            backgammon boards graced weddings
            circumcisions christenings funerals
            everywhere between Damascus and
            Sarajevo Algiers and Batumi

born unshod
   of wealth and privilege
but blessed with
   radiant blue eyes like talismans against evil

he transformed the weary people he met
   into proud sunflowers

he and women
found one another amative
   but perverse fate
      married him to incompatibility
he shouldered forty rancours for every grain of joy

he gave his sons
   the secrets of a noble life
      bread first
         then endurance
            naturally books on all aspects of Creation
               and not least truth in the given word

when death called
   putrefying skin flesh and dignity
this man fragrant with mint
   strode off
      uncrushed
        undefiled
          unwavering

MOTHER
wild marigold of Cuenca
winnowed
from the soot of autos-da-fé
to Macedonia

robbed of childhood
protecting mother from father
with a gun
robbed of adolescence
whilst painting with one hand
and composing with the other
robbed of adulthood
when plucked off Mount Hortiatis
for marriage in Istanbul
and robbed of a lifetime
as Nazi hordes
incinerated the very soul of Salonica
in concentration camps

how could you have
embraced
    a good husband
        tenderly
fed
    uncurdled milk
        to needy sons
trusted

friends who plundered the rosewater in your
heart
    but never soothed the devastation it concealed
how could you have
breathed
    when your sister's skull
      stared at you from a pile of skeletons
        in Birkenau's Crematorium 2

illness and death
were your heroes
and doctors and mediums
your lovers
how could we have healed you
mother dear mother
we who lived to make you live
when you kept spitting out life
in brave madness
as if it were carrion

HISTORY
will forget him
it will forget her too
History is human
History favours
only
the victor
never

the vanquished
never even
the survivor

But the Earth
will redeem them
Earth never forgets her children
Earth will give them
restorative soil
thick and sweet and plentiful

Historiography

Here is a tree.
Her roots cure the ague.
Her leaves heal wounds.
Her berries clean blood that has been poisoned.
Her pith washes the eye of everything that blinds it.
Here is a tree.
She stands to witness the desolation.
She stands to defy
blizzards, hurricanes, droughts and sandstorms.
She stands, a streak of rainbow,
in Adam's lightless universe.
She stands, deathless, even when her children die.
Here is a tree.
Her bark records the chronicles of good and evil.
Her seed plants the next generation.
Her wood empowers reincarnation
by embracing the fire.
She is the Tree of Life.
The Wheel of Time.
Saramama.
Mother.

I need Eros by my side

yesterday
full of sperm
I mocked death

and sailed across borders
to inseminate the world
as the gods have instructed us

today
desperately clinging to old bones and wasted muscles
I plead with death

the voyage home takes longer
the gods didn't tell us that

how can
life
be complete
if it can't return
to the source

but
the source
is cloud-hidden
or maybe
lies in another galaxy

to find it
I need
Eros
by my side
and
genitals renewed
and
more time

I need
nothing less than forever

Manku Yupanqui

He is
the water that quenches the gods
the fire that cleanses the past
He is
the earth where the spirit grows
the sky that shepherds the stars
He is
the eagle who husbands the sun
the puma that hurls rainbows
He is
the pure milk of a man's eruption
the kiss that opens a woman's legs
He is
the hope born today
the stone that will build tomorrow

A vision

Last night
I had a vision
a new vision
as old as time

a vision
without knives
without guns

a vision
conquering famine
conquering drought

a vision
healing wounds
healing sickness

a vision
untouched by barbed wire, prisons, windowless
cells
untouched by disappearances

a vision
beyond treacherous couplings

beyond rejections
a vision
liberated from separations
liberated from the death of love

I had a vision
last night
when the world was
you and I and our child

You do not want us to die unsalted

Now that a man no longer feels the air
enfolding him
like his woman

now that a woman no longer feels the earth
smiling in her womb
like a flower

now that a child no longer feels the water
rocking him
like a lullaby

now that the people no longer feel the fire
quickening their limbs
like love

we know
life has lost
its salt

we know, too,
dear God,
you do not want us to die
unsalted

so here we are
spreading ourselves
on
the wind
the rock
the spring
the sun
when we rise again
we shall rise
as
breath
land
river
hearth

Ballad of the immigrant

tell me
fair woman
tell me
you couldn't eat
yesterday
you couldn't walk talk work
or watch television
tell me
you didn't want
to wash away my smell
yesterday

tell me
pure white woman
this immigrant
this alien
this pariah
is like any other man
even like your pukka citizens
– hungrier maybe –
but you don't mind that
it's a hunger that makes you wet all day
every day

tell me
Western rose
I, the untouchable,
inhabit your cloudless eyes
since yesterday

or
if it will save your pride
say that
as a believer
in
equality
freedom
democracy
human rights
feminism
you're being liberal
indeed charitable

say anything
I don't care
untouchables
know
how to feed on
crumbs

The dead mother

The grave
delivered her
My mother is reborn

She is primary matter now
There is eternity in her dust
It swirls with serenity not pain

She has survived life
She has escaped desolation
She is young, sultry, carefree

See how she paints a landscape
or defiantly plays *rebetika* instead of Chopin
See how she prepares a festive table

She could be my daughter
She is my daughter
She has returned home safely

Look at my father
One of the just men, standing by her side
He is young yet looks ancient
He could be my son

He is my son
He, too, has returned home safely

My mother's table is ready
She feeds the souls of ancestors and progeny
My Mother is Mother Earth now

Odysseus

year after year
he survived
the wars

and struggled
many more years
to reach home

home had turned
to rubble
wife and children
shadows on stone walls

he fled
seeking a place
where he could raise
a new hearth
as Nature insists

he knocked on
neighbouring states
fat paragons
they forbade him entry
fat is for the avaricious only

he approached
distant countries
skinny mendicants
they chased him away
the famished never share

he drifted
toward
the sun
the rainbow
the stars
the icebergs
on lucky days
he followed
a motherly river
a fatherly wind
the rain
the snow
the migrating birds

deserts welcomed him
smelted him down with wisdom
he became a prophet
pious men seized him
and trepanned him
with crowns of thorns

polar regions welcomed him
put a bone into his penis
he became a bear
men with factories
dug a hole in the firmament
and melted the ice

rainforests welcomed him
decked him with miraculous plants
he became a healer
eaters of gold and silver
set the undergrowth on fire

mountains welcomed him
fixed him with wings
he became an eagle
men with electronic devices
shot him down from the skies

seas welcomed him
gave him flippers and the lilt of dolphins
he became a leviathan
men in ships
harpooned him

Eden welcomed him
taught him
the meaning of good and evil
he became a judge

men who juggled with nuclear waste
irradiated him

he escaped to an abandoned woman
she gave him breast
sheltered him between her legs
men frightened of love
stuffed her vagina with stones

he found refuge with bands of children
strengthened their chests
taught them ancient resolve
men preparing Armageddon
shot them all in the back

he crawled back to his old home
and there on the rubble
by the shadows on the walls
men who loved God country and strong leaders
quartered him
for crimes against humanity

thereafter
none dared fraternize with him

he had become
the stranger
the other

the alien
he had become
you
he
she
we

me

For Tony

Chronicles
remember
only
tyrants and assassins
swords and arrows
gunpowder and cannon
defoliants flame-throwers and missiles
and occasionally to dupe us
a verse from Homer
a scene from Shakespeare
a hue from Da Vinci
a ray of light from Rembrandt
a few chords from Mozart, Schubert and the three Bs

But a friend
ah, a friend
a friend
this friend
remembers
your footsteps on earth
your courage in unknown territories
your hand which always strokes never strikes
a friend
this friend

remembers
your beautiful soul
now immortalized on canvas by a prodigious
painter

Miracle woman

I exhorted reason
to forget my age.

Her face upon my face,
we braided our breaths.
She embedded herself in me,
I embedded myself in her.

My pigeon cooed
as if he had been nesting in her haven forever.
She nurtured him ardently.

Time stood deathless.

Freed from life's dungeons
at long last,
naked in flesh and soul,
I had found my rose,
my life's meaning.

I said:
'I give you all that I really am.
I worship your flesh and spirit
with all the goodness in me.'

She said:
'That's all I want.'

Still time stood deathless.

Her radiant eyes
soothed
the scars
of my long years.

I said:
'I can't have enough of you.'
She said:
'Nor I of you.'

I said:
'Sages say
bodies don't lie.
Now I know what that means.'
She said:
'Bodies bless us –
given a chance.'

I drank her nectar
and proclaimed the only truth I knew:
'I love your cunt!
Here lives your Self.
Here lives my Self.

You are my miracle,
my woman!'

Letter from Bosnia, Rwanda, Kosovo, Chechnya, Darfur ...

these are
our birthrights:
    embraces
    daily bread
    work
    sun
    moon
    children
    freedom
    peace
    sanctity
    soul
    god

and these:
    word
    language
    stories
    speech
    memories

and these, too:
    running rivers

amorous valleys
bosom-soft sands
singing forests
echoes across ancient mountains
histories on ancestral stones

and, not least:
deaths that do not humiliate
burials in uncharred earth
judgements in immaculate waters

instead
we get:
tyrants
show-trials
dungeons
bullets
gallows
deportations
flames
plagues
death-pits

For Nina

*On the occasion of her sixtieth birthday,
1 December 2003*

A few truths
from this aging Turk,
my Nin

You are
the sea that gave me life
the earth that suckled me
the cedar that offered me shade
the breeze that carried me everywhere

You are
bread and figs
spring-water and wine
the *oud* and soul-laden songs
culture and language

You taught me
how never to throw stones
how to offer open hands instead of fists
how to winnow courage from the aether
how forgetness is better than forgiveness

You are
– if you still need reminding –
the breath
that gives
the only meaning
to my existence

Linguacide

when a writer is killed
language
loses one of its words

when all writers are killed
there will be
no words left
no language

only
dictators
racists
nationalists
zealots of war
false prophets

only
the worship of death

Tomorrow

Yesterday, the poet al-Ma'ari, told us,
there were two kinds of leaders:
those with brains and no religion;
and those with religion and no brains

yet many people somehow survived
there were still
the skies
the sun
the sea
mountains and forests
love of life and wisdom to create
and myths and prophecies
that promised clement times

Today, unquiet souls warn us,
leaders have congealed into one kind:
those with no religion and no brains

yet the people strive to survive
and
the skies
the sun
the sea

mountains and forests
love of life and wisdom to create
are still here,
defiant
and myths and prophecies
of clement times
are still remembered

Tomorrow, the unborn will say
there are
no skies
no sun
no sea
no mountains and forests
no love of life and no wisdom to create
and myths and prophecies
of clement times
have been effaced
because
there are no people left

Farewell gift

On the death of my wife and soul, Nina

Just before you departed,
my Nin,
you gave me a unique gift,
the only gift that might empower this survivor
to survive.

When Death reached for you,
brave soul that you were,
you faced it.
'It's a wasp,'
you yelled.
'A wasp, of all things!'
You never tolerated wasps,
despised them as 'predators', 'carrion-eaters'.
Whereas you loved bees.
'Devoted to their Queen,'
you extolled them,
'as my Mussy is to me.'

Later, as the wasp buzzed
around your still vibrant curly hair,
you strained to chase it away.

I was holding your hand tightly.
Confounded that, for once in your life,
you were afraid.
Tears convulsed me.
You had seen
the dust awaiting you.
And there was nothing I could do to give you succour.

You rebuked me:
'The wasp! Mussy, get rid of it!'

I spun my arms.
I struck the wall,
in pathetic mime,
to assure you
I had killed it.

You weren't fooled.
My destiny: to fail you.

Swiftly, the wasp settled on you.
You stopped breathing.
I kissed your forehead,
oh, so many times …
'Breathe, Nin!' I pleaded,
'Keep breathing …
'Don't die …
'Please don't die …'

You heard me.
Even as Death stung your heart,
you heard me.
(Or so I will always believe.)
You started breathing again.
Four, maybe five times.
Gentle breaths,
gentlest of breaths.
As on that September evening,
thirty-four years ago,
when we first met and gaped at each other
in wonderment.

Then no more breaths.
You had given me your last.
And given it lovingly.
True to yourself,
as ever.

Your farewell gift to me.

Now, those four five breaths
inhabit me.
and multiply.
Now, every breath I take
is your breath.

Finally

Old age now.

Time of
impaired mobility
wayward faculty
end of poetry

Time to
lie down
and appraise

I've tried to be a good man
knowing I'd always fail
but
I have loved
freely
women men and children
and never demanded
their love
in barter

Time to
lie down
and wait
for the dust
but to keep on loving
while waiting.

Acknowledgements

The rose is one of Nature's greatest miracles. It epitomizes love. And those who embrace love find their lives strewn with petals. They would be blessed as I have been with:

My family, my pillars: Rachel Sievers and Hamish and Zara MacGillivray; Ceki, Viviane, Deborah and Yael Farhi; Eric, Danièle and Nathaniel Gould; Jessica Gould; Phil, Rachel, Samuel, Joshua, Kezia and Joseph Gould; Emmanuel, Yael, Noam, Amit and Adi Gould; Guy, Rebecca, Ela and Uri Granot; Sara, Christopher, Sean and Elli Coil; Nicole Farhi and David Hare; Dennis and Elizabeth Hull.

My twin-souls in the Heavens: Asher Fred Mayer; Mai Ghoussoub; Anthony Masters; Tomek Mirkowicz.

Purveyor of insights into the mysteries: Barry Proner.

My brilliant and devoted editors: Lynn Gaspard, Mitchell Albert and Dide Siemmond.

My friends and mentors: Alev Adil; Selim and Nadia Baruh; Peter Day; Rio and Karen Fanning; Elaine Freed; André and Salwa Gaspard; Maggie Gee and Nicholas and Rosa Rankin; Talat Halman; Richard McKane; Christopher and Christa New; Rebecca O'Connor; Sharon Olinka; Saliha Paker; Donné Raffat; Maureen Rissik; Elizabeth Rosen-Mayer; Anthony Rudolf; Nicholas Sawyer and Juliet Wedderburn; Hazem Saghie; Ros Schwartz; Burhan Sönmez; Martin Tucker.

My kindred spirits near and far: Ergun and Rengin Avunduk; Tricia Barnett; Mevlut Ceylan; Attila and Ayşem Çelikiz; Ian and Anthea Davidson; Rajko and Branko Djuric; Ahmad Ebrahimi; Semra Eren-Nijhar and Indirjit and Ilayda Nijhar; Bensiyon Eskenazi; Saime Göksu-Timms and Edward Timms; Emil Goldenberg; Andrew Graham-Yooll; Agop and Brigitte Hacikyan; Bracha Hadar; Nina Kossman; Julian and Karen Lewis; Robin and Sallie Lloyd-Jones; Easterine Iralu Kire; Robina Masters; Naomi May; Faith Miles; Julita Mirkowicz; Richard and Ceinwen Morgan; Ayşe and Mehmet Önal and Şafak Pavey; David Picker; Lucy Popescu; Paula Rego; Esti Rimmer; Hazel Robinson; Carole Seymour-Jones; Evelyn Toynton; Enis Üser; Rod Wooden.

My agents: Jessica Woollard, Jemma McDonagh and all at the Marsh Agency.

Members of my dedicated "family" at Saqi Books/ Telegram: Amin Al-Issa; Charlotte Allen; Ashley Biles; Rabii Fatihi; Chloe Gill-Khan.

Many of the poems in this collection first appeared in their original form in the following books, literary journals and other publications:

Agenda
First Commandment
Ultimatum
Ballad of the immigrant

Another Day Has Westered
Renunciation

Children of the Rainbow
Historiography

Confrontation
At the doors of a brothel
Claridges, London
Istanbul under the rain

Cruig Festival Review
Time of the rodents

European Judaism
About death – II
About death – IV
Letters to Asher
Rebel
Ties of blood

Evansville Review
Auld lang syne
Saturnalia
Victual
On strawberry beds
Tiredness

Exiles
Partings

Frank
Leaving Istanbul

International PEN Writers in Prison Committee Newsletter
Linguacide

Jewish Quarterly
About death – I
A hungry queue
The dead mother

Journey through the Wilderness
The libertine's song
Royal guest
Journey's start
Manku Yupanqui
Mother
There were days
A vision
You do not want us to die unsalted

Lebanon, Lebanon
Tomorrow

Lucera
I need Eros by my side
Odysseus

Men Card
Seed
Letters to Asher

Modern Poetry in Translation
After Auschwitz
Letter from Bosnia, Rwanda,
Kosovo, Chechnya, Darfur ...
Thirst

The Moth
Miracle woman

North Atlantic Review
About death – I
Redemption
Revenge

Rebwar
About death – III
First Commandment
Ballad of the immigrant

*Reflections on the Universal
Declaration of Human Rights*
Armoured men

Voices within the Ark
Profanity
Luck
Paths to God
Thirst
Chinese whispers

Young Turk
Forget traditions
The dowser